Exits, Desires, & Slow Fires

j.r. rogue

Exits, Desires, & Slow Fires

For My Rebels

Today I Was Hit

with the overwhelming
urge to pack a bag & jump in my car
to see you one last time.
Our real one last time has come & gone.
It wasn't bittersweet.
Instead it was laughter.
It was laughter because we
thought we had more time.
We didn't feel the finality.
I feel it now, but I'm too afraid to
ask you if you feel it, too.
Do you?
Maybe it won't hurt if
you see it the same way.
Today I was hit with this simple
& knowing sadness.
This knowing I will never
know your lips again.
Knowing we will never know
what we could have been.
Today I was hit with something
& the truest way to say
it is to just say it simply:

I miss you.

Pretty Puppet Palms

Tell me you're sorry so we can
both try on the lie.
You're deliberate, we both know it,
so let's stop pretending.
You mean to light me up.
I'm all pressed knees
& red breast.
I'm all shallow breath
& bedroom eyes.
I'm all the
things you want me to be.

Let Me Just Say This Now

because I have to say something.
Because I want you to wonder something.
I want you to wonder
if you'd be better off with me than her,
even if it's just a fleeting thought,
a blink of an eye.
I want to plant that thought there
& I want to know that for one
moment you were mine again.
Even if it was only in
your mind
& mine.

"I Told You So."

I can hear it over & over
in my ears,
in the skipping of my heart.
He collects pretty little poets
& places them in his pocket.
A light one. A dark one.
The wrong one. The right one.
I saw it all. I bit my tongue.
How many stanzas have been
written about the green of his eyes?
How many letters will we use
when we whisper of
the taste of his lips?
The ones that lie.
The ones that hide & keep quiet.

"I told you so."
I wrote it down over
& over on my palm
as I flew his way
against better judgment.
He broke one heart to
touch mine.
Then he kept me on
the line as he pulled
a new one
into his bed, still stained with me.
Their pretty little poses
with him always give it away.

Their pretty little prose, too.
He lies with those green eyes,
but the truth always
finds a way.

They Say You've Got A Thing For Me

& I just don't see it.
You're all wander & drive.
All girls falling at your feet.
I'm too far away & I'm a one-night
stand that neither of us regret but neither
of us asked to see each other again
& that has to mean something.

Or more specifically it means nothing.

I sometimes remember the
night I told you about all the
bad things my father did to me.
How I told you I didn't believe in soulmates
or happily-ever-afters.
How you told me about the girl you lost,
& that I remind you of her.
How I told you that in another life I
could have really fallen in love with you.

I barely know you but
I'm always telling
you everything I can't tell the rest.

They say you've got a thing for me,
& they're too afraid to say they
think I've got a thing for you, too.

If You've Ever Written About Me

I ask you late at night, phone
gripped tight like a lifeline,
if you've ever written about me.
& you tell me yes.
I ask if I can hear it.
& you tell me no.
But the next morning I hear your song.
We are less scared of each other then.
When the sun is awake to watch us.
I spend all day tearing the words apart.
What you say is for me, cannot be for me.
Her eyes are blue, mine are not.
Her legs are long, mine are not.
She is a song, I am a night terror.
You're better at this than I am.
My poems are shallow
graves that give me away.
One glance & the reader can see your foot
sticking out from the black dirt.
I don't have the strength to bury you
the way you always do me.
Let's just be honest & true.

The idea of me & the idea of you
look better together anyway.

I Often Wonder At The Kind Of Man You Are

to be so wanting of something that
does not belong to you.
I used to get sidetracked
by the side of your mouth,
by the way your teeth grazed
your lips when you laughed.
You make me want to lie about my age.
This poem wasn't supposed
to be about you,
but this is what my life is now.
I am all *maybe* & *what if* & *can I go back?*
I wonder what I would sound like
if you turned me into a song.
You reminded me last Tuesday
that my palms
are always ice when I touch you.
You've thawed something inside of me
but the reward is not for you yet.
I am not for you yet.

He's Writing Poetry About Her

in ways he never could for me,
I imagine.

I imagine,
but I don't know.

I can't bring myself to
face the truth of it all.

That she was the heroine
& I was just a plot device,
the almost-ex,
the *before his forever.*

Romances Me

I am caught on the
hook of his song, the hook
of his finger in
my lace.

He will not love
me the way he loved her,
I'll make sure of it.
Give me less, I deserve it.

His humor is what reels me in,
tender tones erased by
smoke ring laughter.
It's the only time he quiets.

He is caught in the
hook of my story,
some lie I've pulled from
the depths.

Gotta make sure
he still romances me.
Gotta make sure he
still wants to cross state lines.

I'm Sorry I Was So Drunk That Night

that we talked it up & I walked it off a cliff.
That it was more about getting over him
& nothing about getting to know you.
I'm sorry I didn't map your body,
that I just closed my eyes & pulled you inside.
I'm sorry I wore red & I was
nothing but *go,*
get it over with,
help me forget.
I'm sorry I stole your shirt,
that I didn't let you hold me.
I'm sorry you never had a chance in hell.
I'm sorry you still think of me.

We Should Have Spent The 4th Of July Together

I like to place that sentence on my tongue.
Weigh the text,
the desperation,
the manipulation.
I'm unsure of the difference now.
I'm not sure what I mean by it,
but I think about it sometimes.

Last night I tried to pull a song
from beneath my flesh.
Some rib I don't need.
They say I was once a rib
pulled from man,
but I just don't know
about all that.

I want to pull something
from myself sweet,
less sinful than this
skin I walk around in.

You tell me the best songs bring
grown men to their knees.
I think of the night you fell to your own,
tasted me & became a feral thing.

I liked you then.

We should have spent the 4th of July together.

This Is Another Poem About You

& I know what you're thinking.
I'm as tired of writing about you
as you're tired of reading about you.
You never hurt me so this is just some
safe place I like to visit from time to time.
You have this mouth that I can't get over
& the things that come from it...
                    you know what you're doing to us.

I know you think it's the only
weapon you have,
but I've felt your hands &
I know what you look like on clean
sheets with nothing but
the street lights on you.

This is another poem about you
& we both know it won't be the last.
I don't think you want it to be the last.

All The Shaky Sounds

He leaves his insecurities
on when he opens his door
& takes my coat.
I buried mine so deep
he pushes himself inside of
me ten minutes later
looking for them but we both know
he will never find them.
He wants to get points for trying,
& I'll give them, sure.
He tries to hold my hands
against his headboard,
above my waterfall hair, but I pull away
because that's too close to cute.
I still pull him closer because he isn't
close enough to hurt me & I want to
pretend he can so I can get off.
I pull his ball cap away when the
street lights hit his profile
& find the vulnerability he hides in there.
He tries to distract me with teeth
grazing pulse points
but I've spoiled it for myself
so we try to drown out the noise
with hushed sighs & nails dug into thighs.
He writes songs about all the shaky sounds
he can recall from our fourteen
one-night stands.
I play them through the speakers

standing at attention,
fighting for attention,
behind a pile of books on my desk
I promised myself I'll read but never will.
I promised him that
one morning I wouldn't
leave before he wakes
& there is something about
the way he kisses my temple &
pretends to believe my lie that makes me
hope I'll stay one of these days.

You're A Cautionary Tale

Your brother came by.
He looks so much like you,
& that scares me.
I'm scared he will shadow your footsteps.
I'm scared he will romance
all that you have done.
I'm scared he will fall for me, too,
& I'm scared I won't push him away.

I feel like you're more of a
ghost in this town
than the legend you thought you'd be.
You're a cautionary tale,
they won't let your name
fall from their lips.
I'm collateral damage,
I pull pity from their pupils.

Your sister came by, too,
with your things,
with a sorry, because
you didn't leave one behind.
She thinks you're a
coward but she won't say it.
I think you're a coward, too,
but I'm not afraid of what that means.

I hope you never come back.
I hope you never come back.

I Like The Old You Better

than the one I am sitting with here now,
but I never tell you that.
Or I tell you that, but you don't listen.
Or I tell you that, & you say
"You made me this way"
& I can't argue with that.
I liked you better when you liked me less
& that's pretty sick,
but at least it's honest.
Honest is the last thing we do anymore
& I wonder what our paper faces think
of each other. If they're in love with
each other the way the real you & me
can never seem to be.
I like the old me better than
the one I give you,
but she is too dirty for you.
Too real.

All The Ways One Writer Misses Another Writer

The writer tells the
boyfriend it meant nothing.
The days she loved the
other writer meant nothing.
It wasn't even love, really,
she just wrote it that way.
The metaphors they passed from
mouth to mouth to muscle to
moan meant nothing.
The writer tells the boyfriend she wrote
the other writer up.
He is, in fact, not a tender lover.
His long hair, the way it felt
between her fingertips,
she can't remember it.
She doesn't pull out their photo,
the only one taken together,
from time to time.
She doesn't pull out the last letter he sent.
The one about the way the surf tastes in
September.
The one about all the ways one writer
misses another writer.
The writer tells the boyfriend she
never thinks of the other writer.
She never misses him.

The boyfriend tells the writer
he believes her.
The boyfriend can lie, too.

Unlucky 13

The secrets that had
secluded themselves
near my waist had somehow
become towering cities.

Unlucky number 13.
That's what I called you.

You were the only one I wanted
to walk
in my streets.
The only one I wanted to
whisper into the alleys
& backdoor bars
that were the truth of my map.

Tourists
never belonged there.
You were never meant
to stay.

The Tidal Wave

You, the light storm.
You, the confession.
You, the vibrant lips.
You, forgiveness folded into me, unwanted.

I am undeserving, repenting, repeating
the days that drove you away.

How do I become the tidal wave?
How do I wash this cold cry from my veins?

Hope In A Helium Tank

Every night,
at a quarter 'til three,
he came home
sweat stained
& glowing
with a body
I wanted to live in.

He put his lips on
my temple
& lower
& lower
     & he was
       my lover.

He grabbed my hand
& we laughed
up the stairs
& he took me higher
& he reminded me of
who I was.

He Should Have Been More Careful With Me

It's there,
in the soft moments I cannot touch.
Gentle reminders that
I was nothing, nothing special to him.
That thieving lips
linger only because I let them.
He fell three days in,
lying to himself but
always careful with me.

> *He should have been*
> *more careful with me.*

The bitter mark left on my heart is
nearly faded away
these days.

> *I forgive him.*

Divorce yourself from that spot
you fixate on.
The ceiling fan above your bed
does well to hypnotize,
but I'm still here.

> *I'm not inside him anymore.*

Know that the love has
flown back.
Know that I want
only beauty for him.

> I hope you know this poem is
> nothing but lies.

It's Going To Hit You Violently

You're going to reach for the closest
human, railing, ripcord, trigger.
You're going to see a picture
of his cheek close to hers.
Her blushing smile will be warm
to his flesh & you're going
to remember the way it felt
under your fingertips when you shook
quietly under the
light tiptoeing
into his downtown apartment,
under his tender attention to
every swell & sigh you created.
You're going to forget for a
moment that this is the woman you
worried over & this is the
woman he said was just a
friend & this is the subject
he changed & this is the woman you
felt foolish over.
You're going to remember
that he told you he had never felt the
way he felt with you with anyone else
& you're going to remember
the way his hair touched his
shoulders & your shoulders
& the way he shuddered when
you told him you loved him &
he returned the words in such a wanting

whispering way that you
never had a reason to doubt that this
was a truth he was afraid to
know but was dying to live.

It's going to hit you below the belt.
You're going to reach for the
closest stand-in lover you can
find & you're going to make
a home in their body &
you're going to pretend your
childhood memories are hung
in his chest & you skinned your knee
tripping over the curve of his arm
& you have always been here &
there is no reason to grab a
roll of tape at the checkout to wrap
'round & 'round your heart because
it is not broken & you are not a nomad.
You have always lived & loved
this stand-in-lover &
he is the one standing here so
why can't everyone stop staring at you?
You're going to delete the screenshots
of the texts he sent you fourteen months
ago that you were trying to

pretend didn't exist in your digital history
& you're going to wrap
your fingers around your
skull & the pressure is going to lessen
a little but not enough because
there is no delete button for the screenshots

in your head of the way he stepped
out of the shower
& the way he smiled
around his toothbrush when
you winked at him from over
his shoulder into the mirror
of your cramped little bathroom
& you didn't mind because
you couldn't walk by him without
brushing your body against his anyway.

It's going to hit you from behind.
When your friend screws on
sympathetic eyes & gently
touches your shoulder because
she tried to tell you she saw
something there between
them & she tried to warn you
but he said it was a ridiculous notion,
& she was half the woman
you were & he would never
run away & now you're the
fool in a one-bedroom
apartment & she is in the
bed you bought
& she is friends with the
friends you shared &
they all knew but they
were too afraid to tell you.
You're going to chain the
color of his eyes to everyday objects
& you're going to
call those colors liars &

you're going to bury them
in the backyard with the
cologne bottle he left behind.
You're going to chant your
name as it is over & over.
You're going to un-memorize
the way his last sounded
with your first & you're
going to convince yourself
they never went together anyway.

It's going to hit you from the past.
You're going to see stars it'll hit
you so hard.
You're going to scramble numbers & dates.
You're going to remember
the way the shore sounded
different from his tiny bedroom
window & the way his friends
made you feel
welcome in a strange land.
You're going to forget she
fell for him on that same
shore & you're going to
make up stories about his
shaky hands holding her
phone snapping her
silhouette into a
permanence that will be
the start of their story told
over drinks with the friends
that made her feel welcome
in a strange land.

You're going to love him in reverse.
Hold onto this moment
& hold onto the closest human,
railing, ripcord, trigger.
You're going to pass little
white hatchbacks & you're going
to wander into their lane a
little before you stop yourself & toss
the paperback he sent you
out the window.
You're going to rip the
phone off the wall for
dramatics, for theatrics,
for nostalgia.
You're going to write him
into every poem &
you're going to rip him
from
    every
       single
          song.

Not The Real Me

Let's be honest. This isn't me leaving him.
He's never had me, not really, so it shouldn't
really
hurt. I'm half-woman,
half-paper-doll with him.
There is this mania deep
within that I am unable to
place into his palms.
I've been retracing my steps.
Trying to find something
comforting to offer him.
It turns out I've done this
with every other man.
Every significant man.
Every one-night stand.
Every damn one.
A close friend told me the other
day that I'm a runner.
God, she's so right.
They aren't allowed to have me,
these men who
have loved me. Not the real me.
When it ends, &
it always does, I can hold onto
this sad little truth.
That they never really lost
me because they never
really had me.

I am my own to break.
I am my own.

Alone

I keep the last notes you ever wrote me
paper clipped together in the top drawer
of my desk.
I pull them out from time to time,
run my fingers
over the edges but I never read them.
I can't cry in front of others,
& I never let
myself be alone anymore,
not since you left.

I can still see the words in my mind.
Your handwriting was always shit,
but the red ink was always telling.

We bled. We bled every day for each other.
You, in poetry. Me, internally.

I'm not sure how my hands work to pull
out that worn paper.
How I move about each day.
How my heart still beats. I bled out when
you whispered goodbye into my hair.

You couldn't handle the way I hated myself.
The way I shied away from cameras &
never pulled down the visor in your old
mustang because I'd be punched in the face
with my own reflection.

You were so close to making me believe your
lies.
That I was beautiful & true & everything
you needed to forget the way the venom
women before me
had worn you down.

I never let myself be alone anymore.
Not since you left.
I am always alone.

My Love Is Blue Fire, Red Lies

In this life, you are Poseidon.
You are drowning instinct.
You are the ocean I never wash out.
You are in the air,
in the drapes,
scent in eyelash,
mythical creature.
You are blonde hair & that scar
on your lip is drawing
me to the cliff's edge.
In this life, you are gold glimmer,
the place my palm reaches.
I am empty & empty
& an endless dripping faucet.
I am, in this life,
fused to your smile,
your lie,
your leaving.

I Want You Ivory Skin

underneath my harp string hands to see
if my mute ears will awaken.
I need a beat, a rhythm, in my
casket-colored skin.
It's empty there,
now that you no longer
find your way in.
Your voice in concert with my
sideways smile—
tell me where I can buy a ticket
for that show.
Tell me where I have to go,
to find our maps crossed
& our music married.

You're all I hear.
anymore.

Games In Which We Rename Everything

This is healing.
This is salvation.
This is coming home.
I'm not one of the good guys.

If the walls do not crumble inward,
sleep in my bed, is it really
the end of all things?

This is your bottom lip.
This is where good girls go to die.
This is not your father's legacy.
I'm one of the lovers you should hold onto.

If you break my heart
& I still smile,
was it ever love at all?

I Haven't Heard From You In Weeks

I checked the junk mail folder in my
email this morning to see if maybe
I missed you, if maybe you slipped in
& you're wondering why you
haven't heard from me either.

I want you to tell me you love me,
even though I can't say it back.
I'm selfish like that,
but that's never been news to you.

You're in love with the feeling
you get when you free fall.
When you are empty.
That's why you latch on to me.

On August 5th, two years ago,
I think you wanted to say it the real way.
You ran your thumb along my jaw
& you gave me a new smile.

I count & catalog each one you deliver,
but this one was so so new,
a little blue, a little less lost.

I haven't heard from you in weeks.
I wish I could accept the answer in that.

Sunday Coffee & Second Chances

I put the coffee on.
I don't drink it, but he does.
& I am trying to be a better lover.
Less lost in my own drowning pool.
Less clenched fist.
Less red jaw, tangled apologies.
I run my thumb along his hairline
as I pass him in the dining room.
I press my toes to the top of his
feet under the table.
Catch his eyes, twice.
I am learning to be a better lover.
I am learning to know less of leaving.

Side Character

I don't remember
the moment you pushed into me—
                                    needful.
The first press of your lips to mine—
                        hungry.
I was drowning the remains
of my soulmate in vodka & violets.
Fresh salt on my cheek
left by his vague goodbye crept
up from the tomb
I buried it in last summer.
I do remember I plucked at your
charm, pulled it from the side of your mouth,
savored the bite to it.
Ran my hands through your
hair & tried to find
the vulnerability you aimed to hide.
You're nothing special on paper.
A side character, cheap for a laugh,
pretty for the pupils.
They won't write you into the review,
they don't want to, they've forgotten you.
But babe, don't pout,
don't look so half-masted.
Join me in the laugh.
They are not my master,
their ship is not their own.
They can't make me
un-need you,

they can't make the warmth
of your breath not home.

Hummingbird

He was twenty-four years old
& he told me he had died twice.
One shallow death, one deep.
At thirteen & twenty-one.
He came back each time a little smaller.

I never cared for math or right angles.
Words were currency.
Then there he was in my grey bedroom,
the floor to ceiling windows letting the rain
paint us the way we really were.

His legs were stretched
out on my sheets & his back
straight against the wall.
He put each hand behind my legs,
where they bend & take me places,
& he pulled me to him.

He told me about
resurrections & those fools
in his life who didn't

wait for the second act.

I placed my palm on his chest,
it beat faster than a
hummingbird when I was close,
& I tried to calm my own,

to hide the "I love you"
caught in my throat.

Where You Are

I often wonder about us.
You, the one I am meant for.
You, the one who sees me.
I fear we are not meant to be.

I'll settle down with a good man.
He'll make love to me every night
& share his dreams with the
curve of my neck.

I'll run my fingers in his hair &
feel the safeness his scent pours
into me, during the dark days that
always seem to grip me.

On Sundays he will bring me
breakfast in bed & I will laugh like
a little girl as he takes me in the shower,
while the rain pelts our blue tin roof.

We will have full bellies & full
hearts & a full life that our friends
envy as we joke & tease each other with
drinks in our hands at our monthly card nights.

I'll kiss him every morning.
I'll stare at the ceiling
after he leaves, before
I swing my legs down

to the hardwood floor.
& I'll wonder where you are.

Tabula Rasa

It was a holiday.
A day away from the bump,
& the grind, & the time-clock, & the road.
You let me sleep until nearly noon.
I woke to grape jelly pancakes, my favorite.
The day would be whatever we
needed it to be.
You took off with my plate
& I stripped the sheets from
our bed as I rose,
tossing them in the far corner of
our sweaty room.
We made love in the shower.
You made jokes in the car.
We had gyros for dinner at that
little pizza place
on 4th & came home late to the
howling of our hounds
with arms full up of everything we
didn't need to buy & one thing
we needed to move on.
I ran up the stairs
& dressed our bed with
crisp new sheets.
Ones you didn't make love to her in.
Ones I never cried all over.
Ones I never whispered
deceitful words to him upon.
I threw up the window

& threw out our old linens
& threw away my doubts
that we could be new again.

Hope

We were wrestling on
the couch when you
ripped my new shirt.

For once, it wasn't
the end of the world.

& that has been the
best sign I've seen in
a long time.

Tasted Like Poetry

I often caught him reading
the ink on my skin.
I had chosen each piece carefully.
The poetry of every romantic I would
never be able to touch.

I wanted to tell him
that they would never
compare to the way
his own made me feel.
His voice in my hair,
his breath on the soft
skin of my center as he
kissed me lower & lower.

He liked to linger just an
inch away as I gripped
his sheets & whimpered,
choking on words a shade
less classy than the ones
forever on my flesh.
He swears that I taste like poetry.
Not many days go by that he
doesn't want to devour every word
inside of me that he can't see.

I Could Write For Days About You

I could write for days
on your teeth.
The expanse was
a fright at first.
Like your laugh,
with so many knives,
could swallow
the night whole.
I drummed my fingers on
the steel walls of the train.
Practiced & planned
to press a ballad
into your ivory with
my tiny fingertips.
Listened to your
tongue trick them into
opening wide,
into letting me
devour your stories.
I could write for days about you.

The Cure

California premium
fresh cherries sweeten me.
I spit the seed into the street
& your sweet
lips are a tinge
too red from kissing me.

Pulling me away
from my tattered paperback.
Pulling me away
from my silly somber ways.

You,
yes you, have become the cure
for every damn thing
that ails me.

The Problem With Temptation

He said "I want you,"
& I heard
I'm tired of tiring cover tunes,
I think I could cry a song about you.

He said "I heard you fell in love again,"
& I heard *there's a hook*
in the curve of your back,
let me write us real.

That's the problem with temptation,
it always leads you to me,
& I fiction the truth away.

Pillow Talk

"So my secrets slide out
during pillow talk," I told him.
& my god, he laughed,
something like music.
His eyes went greyscale,
his voice took the stairs,
his hands threw out my dress.
He heard sex.
I spoke intimacy,
bordering countries,
one river flowing into another.
My god, he laughed, &
I couldn't figure out why I didn't care
that he missed the point.
Couldn't see that I would be nailing
"Have you seen this person?" flyers to
power line poles within a week.
Looking for this girl here now,
drowning in his laugh,
throwing her secrets away.
Looking for this girl so
I can cut out her tongue,
learn her some lessons,
maybe just one.

All The Nameless

There's a book on my balcony
with a note tucked inside.
Some letter you wrote to me about
the cold ocean air on your face when
your surfed the northern shore.
The note doesn't say much but I will it to.
All the nameless
back-breaking borderline-giving-in confessions
I begged for.
Did I draw it all out?
No, I never could.
All the nameless, the pleading, the unbelieving.
I wrote it on your ribs at night,
watched the shadows move along your
trembling.
There's a book on my balcony
& some nights I walk out
& muse I'll throw it over,
& I laugh at myself.
Oh, all the nameless gods laugh at me.
But I know they envy me.
For a moment, a human
song like you loved me.

Gooseflesh & Downy Halos

I remember the hairbrush I would leave
on the nightstand.
The one my mother gave me.
You aimed to throw it away, one day.
When your patience was tested & you were
tempted to punish me, just so.
You never did, though.
With me you were half a man
half a cliché.
A Roman
fairytale, told at dawn,
at the set of the moon,
at the brush of my lace
from my blushing thighs.

I remember the hairbrush
I would leave on the nightstand.
I remember the cool ocean air
painting my skin,
gooseflesh & downy halos.

I remember too much of you.
Maybe one day I'll tell the world our story.

Barely

You would hold
my two bare feet
in your calloused
hands on Sundays.
When the rain came,
& the pain came,
& you drew out
the poison
while b a r e l y
moving
        a muscle.

The Worst Kind Of Game

I just wanted to be a kid again,
to make this grownup shit go away.
So I wore a little mermaid shirt to
the airport & tried not to cry.

I failed & you saw it,
so you put the car in park
& kissed me.

I'm still lingering in that moment.

I spent the rest of the car ride
practicing my numbers & letters
again like you do in kindergarten.
The letters wouldn't make up words
that could explain to you how I felt.
& the numbers just counted me closer
to the parking lot & the gate & the plane.

Some days love is the worst kind of game.

Holy Water

I should've told you about the flood.
How he was water & I could never escape.
How I never tried to escape.

They're Taking Bets On Us

On when we will write our names
together in hearts, or some
bullshit like that.
Or maybe just when we will fuck
& forget each other.

That's more us, really,
& they know it.
You say they're hoping
we will save each other.
So they can laugh that they
were there for the game changer.
You being mine or me being yours.

I'm not sure who is more
the villain in this torrid affair.
First glance? I win hands down.
I've got heartache laced into my jaw.

If I'm being honest I spend
most early Saturday mornings
writing about the way you're going
to leave me.

It's such a laugh to sketch
your leaving heel when you
haven't even had the chance to be my *now*.

But you & I both know

this little sickness inside of me is the
part you want to touch the most.

Just Friends

So it turns out we're never
going to be anything
more than a one-night stand.
It's a bitch but maybe a cynic like me can
weave some silver lining into our tale.
Maybe that's a skill I never knew I had.
I think I need you in some
way that I'll never
be able to explain on paper.
You're my confessional.
You're the brutal truth when
everyone else is spoon-feeding me roses.
I never liked to be treated
with kid gloves anyway.
I'm no open book but one look at my cover
& you're whispering my plot twists before
I've had a chance to blow on the ink.
We're never going to be what they're saying
we should be so let's just be whatever the
hell we want to be.
Let's just admit that maybe
we need each other
& that maybe just friends isn't always
such a bad place to land.

So You Think You Know Me

You say we are devil twins,
kindred killers.
You've been googling my symptoms,
trying them on for laughs,
writing your name with mine
in some bubbly heart.
You say I am less like a flower,
more like a sword,
& that's why you need me.
I know you're a masochist,
that you want to be a magician,
but I only like you when I'm drunk
& you can't see what that means.
You think you know me,
but I pray you never do.

J.R. Rogue first put pen to paper at the age of fifteen
after developing an unrequited high school crush &
never stopped writing about heartache.

She has published multiple volumes of poetry
& four novels.

Two of her poetry collections, La Douleur
Exquise & Exits, Desires, & Slow Fires, have been
Goodreads Choice Awards nominees.
To keep up with everything she is working on, join
her Facebook group, Rogue's Rebels, & join
her mailing list for exclusive coupons.

also by j.r. rogue

Novels

Burning Muses
Background Music
Kiss Me Like You Mean It
I Like You, I Love Her

Poetry

La Douleur Exquise
Tell Me Where It Hurts
An Open Suitcase & New Blue Tears
Rouge
Le Chant Des Sirènes
Apus
Letters to the Moon
All Of My Bullshit Truths: Collected Poems
Breakup Poems: Vol 1

Secrets We Told The City
w/Kat Savage

43445549R00041

Made in the USA
Lexington, KY
28 June 2019